the public law supporting mainstreaming:
a guide for teachers and parents

by
a. lee parks
university of idaho

marilyn k. rousseau
university of idaho

thomas n. fairchild
series editor

bart l. miller
illustrator

LEARNING CONCEPTS
2501 N. Lamar Austin, Texas 78705 (512) 474-6911

Library of Congress Cataloging in Publication Data

Parks, A Lee
  The public law supporting mainstreaming

  (Mainstreaming series)
  1. Handicapped children—Law and legislation—United States
  2. Handicapped children—Education—United States.
  I. Rousseau, Marilyn K., joint author.   II. Title
  KS4210.P3   344'.73'0791   77-6778
  ISBN 0-89384-018-1

Learning Concepts
2501 North Lamar
Austin, Texas 78705

In memory of my father, Al Parks, whose
energy and intelligence was an inspiration
to all who knew him.

A. Lee Parks

To LaVerne Graves

Marilyn Rousseau

acknowledgments

We would like to extend our sincere appreciation to a number of people who have helped in the preparation of this manuscript.

For their assistance in reviewing the manuscript:

Tom Fairchild, Editor of the **MAINSTREAMING SERIES,** College of Education, University of Idaho;

Judy Schrag, Director of Special Education, State Department of Education, Idaho;

Linda Gibbs, Regional Resource Consultant, Division of Special Education, State Department of Education, Idaho; and

Mike Orlansky, Instructor, Department of Special Education, University of Idaho.

For their secretarial assistance in the preparation of the manuscript:

Marcy Taylor, Shellie West, and Lee Brydon.

Thanks also to Carolyn Fairchild for cartoon ideas.

preface

In the past, educational needs of exceptional children were met by removing them from the "mainstream" of the regular classrooms, and serving them in a variety of segregated, self-contained, special classes. The trend in the '70's is educating exceptional children in the least restrictive educational setting; that is, as close as possible to their normal peers. This concept of mainstreaming exceptional children has received considerable support from within and outside the educational community. Although self-contained special classes will always be a meaningful alternative for some children, the personal and educational needs of many exceptional children can be better served in the regular class program with the supportive services of ancillary personnel and/or resource room help.

With the emphasis on mainstreaming, the regular class teacher is now expected to meet the needs of exceptional children in his or her classroom along with all the other children in the class. The problem is that most regular class teachers have little or no preparation in the area of educating exceptional children. Regular class teachers need basic information regarding the various exceptionalities and more specifically, practical suggestions which they can employ to enhance the mainstreamed exceptional child's personal and educational development. Teachers also need to be acquainted with the law (P.L. 94-142) that has given the impetus to mainstreaming, and the law's implication for them.

The MAINSTREAMING SERIES was written to fill these needs. Most of the books in the SERIES address themselves to specific areas of exceptionality, allowing teachers to select from the SERIES according to their interest or need. These texts provide information designed to eliminate misconceptions and stereotypes and to improve the teacher's understanding of the exceptional child's uniqueness. Numerous practical suggestions are offered which will help the teacher work more effectively with the exceptional child in the mainstream of the regular classroom. Other texts within the SERIES focus on working with parents, the public law, and developing an individualized educational program for the exceptional child.

Currently, there is a great deal of controversy surrounding the use of categories and labels. The books in the SERIES are organized according to categories of exceptionality because the content within each book is only relevant for a child with a specific handicapping condition. The intent is not to propagate labeling; in fact, labeling children is inconsistent with the philosophy of the SERIES. The books address themselves to behaviors and how teachers can work with these behaviors in exceptional children. The books in the SERIES are categorized—not the children. The books are categorized in order to cue teachers to the particular content for which they might be looking.

There is much truth in the old saying, "A picture is worth a thousand words." A cartoon format was used for each book in the MAINSTREAMING SERIES as a means of sustaining interest and emphasizing important concepts. The cartoon format also allows for easy, relaxed reading. We felt that teachers, being on the firing line all day, would be more likely to read and refer to our material than to a lengthy text filled with theory and jargon. Typical to cartooning is the need to exaggerate, stereotype, and focus on our weaknesses. I sincerely hope the cartoons do not offend any children, parents, or professionals, because that is not the purpose for which they were intended. They are intended to make you think.

I hope you find this book helpful in your work with mainstreamed exceptional children, or with any other children, since they are all special.

THOMAS N. FAIRCHILD
SERIES EDITOR

contents

chapter 1

---

purpose and definitions

PURPOSE OF THE NEW LAW

The Education For All Handicapped Children Act, also known as Public Law 94-142, provides the legal basis for providing educational services in the least restrictive setting.

"Mainstreaming" is the popular term for providing education for handicapped children in the least restrictive environment, that is, educating handicapped children as closely as possible to their normal peers.

The decision to place a handicapped child in a regular class for all or part of the school day will depend on the unique characteristics and educational needs of the individual child.

Mainstreaming for the severely handicapped child might mean removing him/her from an institutional setting to a public school special education program. Mainstreaming for a mildly handicapped child could mean transferring him/her from a self-contained public school classroom to a resource room in which he/she spends part of the school day. The remainder of the day would be spent in the regular class.

It is important for parents and teachers to remember that mainstreaming, as the term is used in this book and others in the Series, does not necessarily mean placement in a regular class. It could mean that the child may be moved from a regular class setting when it is evident that supplemental assistance in that class is clearly not sufficient.

Mainstreaming provides more educational opportunities for handicapped children and helps them avoid the stigma attached to labeling.

In 1975 Congress passed the Education For All Handicapped Children Act. The Act has four major purposes:

1. To assure that all handicapped children have available to them a free appropriate public education. . .

. . .which emphasizes special education and related services designed to meet their unique needs.

A free appropriate public education must meet several criteria:

    a. It must be at public expense with no cost to the parents or guardians of the child;

    b. It must meet the standards set by the state department of education;

    c. It must include appropriate preschool, elementary, or secondary school education; and it must include an individualized educational program.

Other purposes of the law are:

2. To assure that the rights of handicapped children and
    their parents or guardians are protected;

3. To assist states and localities in providing for the education of all handicapped children; and

4. To assess and assure the effectiveness of efforts to educate handicapped children.

This law is consistent with other, similar laws that have been developed during the last five years in several states. It establishes a standard of service to handicapped children that applies to all 50 states. Its purpose is to provide appropriate services to children.

DEFINITIONS

The new law defines several terms. Three terms that parents and teachers should be aware of are:

- handicapped;
- special education; and
- related services.

A *handicapped* child is defined as one who is "mentally retarded, hard of hearing, deaf, speech impaired, visually handicapped, seriously emotionally disturbed, ortho-pedically impaired, or other health impaired, or children with specific learning disabilities, who by reason thereof require special education or related services."

The Act defines *special education* as "specially designed instruction, at no cost to parents or guardians, to meet the unique needs of a handicapped child, including classroom instruction, instruction in physical education, home instruction, and instruction in hospitals and institutions."

Related services means "transportation. . .

. . .and such developmental, corrective, and other supportive services as may be required to assist a handicapped child to benefit from special education, and includes early identification and assessment."

Other supportive services include: speech pathology and audiology, psychological services, physical and occupational therapy, recreation, counseling services, and diagnostic and evaluative medical services.

TIMELINES

It is estimated that approximately one million handicapped children in the United States are not receiving a free, public education.

Many of these children are not in school because of matters such as the religious convictions of their parents, mobility problems, inhabiting very isolated rural settings, and parental embarrassment of handicaps. But there are several children who have been excluded by the public schools. This law was developed to hasten the rate at which handicapped children will have access to public services.

According to this law, each state is to provide a *free appropriate* public education to all children between the ages of 3 and 18 by September 1, 1978. Children ages 3 to 21 are to have these services available to them by September 1, 1980.

As the timeline indicates, priority is given to the younger children (3-5 years of age) and older children (18-21 years of age) because the intent is to provide services to the unserved children first. These children, between 3-5 and 18-21, make up a large part of the unserved population. Another priority is to serve children with severe handicaps who may be receiving either no service or inadequate services.

Some states have laws which prohibit the spending of public funds on children in the 3-5 and 18-21 age ranges. In these states, the timelines will not apply to the education of these age groups; they will apply to children ages 6-18.

Another exception to these timelines has been made in states that are under court order to provide services to children by a different date. States which are working under such court orders are, in most cases, required to meet an earlier deadline than the one set forth in this law. The general intent is not to slow down delivery of services, but to speed them up.

It is unfortunate that such a law was not available sooner. For the present generation of handicapped children it will provide the needed services when these can be of most benefit to the child. Change comes slowly in most societies, as it probably should. Yet children grow surprisingly rapidly; therefore, early identification and prevention are critical. Many handicaps can be remediated much more easily if services are provided when the child is young. Hopefully, we have seen the last generation of handicapped children who will not receive appropriate services.

CHILD IDENTIFICATION

Many handicapped children have been excluded from the public schools and are not receiving an education. Public Law 94-142 requires that each state develop a method to identify, locate, and evaluate handicapped children so that a free appropriate public education can be made available to them.

Some states have developed "Child Find" activities.

CHILD FIND
TURN IN A
KID

These states are using radio and television commercials to inform the public that school districts are looking for handicapped children who are not receiving an education. Other methods of identification include newspaper articles, posters, billboards, and flyers placed in doctor's offices, hospital waiting rooms, restaurants, and other public places.

If you have or know of a handicapped child who is not receiving a free appropriate public education, contact your local school district or the state director of special education.

chapter 2

---

assessment of
handicapped children

This chapter discusses the legal requirements associated with the assessment of handicapped children. The major aspects of the law regarding assessment include requirements for:

- Due process
- Due process procedures
- Comprehensive evaluation
- Protection in evaluation procedures
- Access to student records

DUE PROCESS

What does "due process" mean? Due process means that there are legal procedures *due* to citizens before the state can deny them certain important rights and privileges. It is the right of every individual that these legal procedures (due process procedures) be correctly followed at all times.

According to the 14th Amendment to the Constitution, it is an assumption of *due process* that certain standards of procedural fairness be followed before the state can remove or deny a right or a privilege.

What are the situations that might lead parents to seek some of the procedures *due* to them? And what are these procedures legally owed to parents and children? The following section describes situations as well as due process procedures.

DUE PROCESS PROCEDURES

These are at least three typical situations which might lead parents to seek some, or all, of the legal procedures owed to them:

- School personnel are considering placing a child in a special class.

- School personnel are considering removing a child from a special class.

● School personnel are considering a change of educational programming.

Either the parents or the school may initiate a request to place a child in a special class. Either party may also request that the child be removed from such a class. Some states' laws prohibit the state from initiating due process. You can contact the department of education in your state for information on whether or not they can initiate a due process procedure.

Schools are required to provide the parents with *written notice* whenever the school proposes to initiate or change the identification, evaluation, or educational placement of a child. A notice is also required if the school refuses to initiate or change a program. This written notice keeps parents and guardians abreast of the educational situation of their child. In the past, some parents have not been informed prior to testing or educational placement of their child.

This means that the parents must be given written notice before the child is assessed, labeled, or put into any class other than the one he/she is presently in.

Parents have the right to refuse. . .

. . .as well as to approve any change in their child's educational status. They also have the right to refuse the placement of their child in a special class. From the parents' point of view, nonplacement in a special class may be seen as the most appropriate solution. The important point is that parents should give permission for testing and placement.

This written notice should be in the native language of the parent or guardian if at all possible. In the case of common foreign languages such as Spanish and French it should be possible for most school systems to write the notice in the native language.

It should be emphasized that the parents may raise questions about any or all of the aspects of program development - *identification, evaluation,* or *placement.* It is possible that the parents would be perfectly satisfied with most aspects of the program development but have concerns with others. For example, they may completely agree with all the identification and evaluation procedures but be concerned about the placement recommendation. They may feel that the program is not being conducted in the least restrictive environment for the child.

Should the parents have any complaints about some aspect of identification, evaluation, or placement, they should ask for a school conference. If the problems cannot be resolved they can ask for an *informal due process hearing.* They also have the right to such a hearing if they are not satisfied that their child is receiving a free appropriate education.

Informal due process hearings should be impartial and should not be conducted by an employee of the school system. Parents have the right to:

1. Be accompanied by counsel and by those who have special training in serving the handicapped;

2. Present evidence, confront and cross-examine witnesses, and require them to be present;

3. Receive a written or recorded report of the informal hearing; and

4. Receive a written report of the findings and decisions of the agency conducting the hearing.

Occasionally the parents or the school district may be dissatisfied with the findings of such an informal hearing. In these cases, either party may appeal to the state education agency for a review of the results from the earlier hearing. This hearing should also be conducted by an impartial individual.

If either party objects to the results of the appeal to the state education agency, civil action may be initiated in a state or United States District Court.

Appeal processes often take considerable amounts of time. Educational services for the child should not be discontinued during this process. He/she has the right to remain in the class he/she was in before the legal action began. Of course if the parents and school agree, the child may also be placed in any other educational program pending the results of the appeal process.

If the child does not have parents or a guardian and the state has appointed surrogate parents. . .

. . .these individuals have available to them, on behalf of the child, all due process procedures. This surrogate cannot be an employee of any other educational agencies responsible for the child.

REVIEW

The 14th Amendment to the Constitution has a due process clause which indicates that certain fair procedures must be followed. In regard to P.L. 94-142, parents have the right to written notice in their native language whenever the school proposes to initiate or change a child's:

- classification;
- assessment; or
- educational program.

Parents may support or deny any of these changes in their child's status. The parents have a right to a hearing. Throughout any hearing, whether in the school district, state education agency, state court, or United States District Court, parents have a right to:

- be represented by counsel;
- have professionals present who are trained in serving the handicapped;
- present evidence;
- confront and cross-examine witnesses;
- require witnesses to be present; and
- receive a complete report of the hearing as well as the findings.

COMPREHENSIVE EVALUATION

The Education For All Handicapped Children Act requires that a comprehensive and nondiscriminatory evaluation be provided for the child. In the past it has not been uncommon to find that handicapped children had been placed in special classes on the basis of a single test score obtained by a school psychologist or psychometrist.

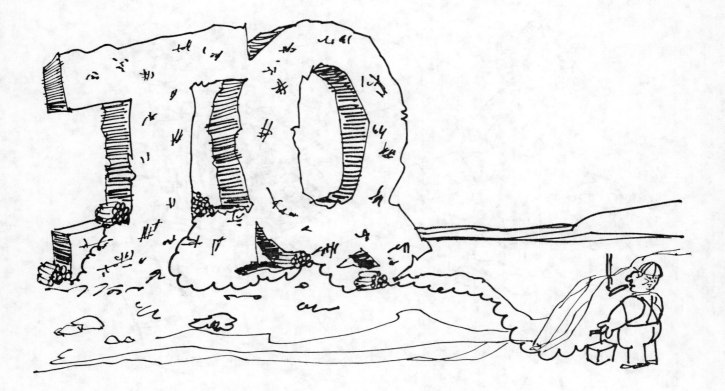

Other tests and evaluations from professionals such as speech and language specialists and physicians had often been lacking. This section discusses the basic components of comprehensive evaluations and suggests ways to achieve compliance with the law.

The law stipulates that no single testing procedure should be used to place a child in a special program. A single test or test score is not sufficient. Testing should be "multi-faceted." This means that testing should involve more than one discipline and more than one test within each discipline.

Evaluation should take into account such factors as: communication skills, educational achievement, physical health and condition, psychological status, and social skills.

Communication skills are usually most appropriately assessed by a speech and communication disorders specialist. This individual might assess the child's ability to properly articulate sounds and to use words to communicate effectively with others. In cases where the child is severely handicapped the assessment might include examining the child's ability to use nonoral communication procedures or devices.

Educational assessment involves the measurement of basic classroom skills in academic or preacademic performance. This assessment should identify the specific skills and deficits of the child. Both standardized tests and criterion-referenced tests can be used for this purpose. Standardized tests are used to compare the child to a norm group. These tests ask the question, "How well does the child perform on this task as compared to other children his/her age?" Criterion-referenced tests compare the child with him/herself.

These are essentially lists of important, basic skills upon which teachers base their instruction. These tests ask the question, "What basic skills does this child demonstrate?"

Assessment of physical health and condition typically involves a physical examination of the child to detect general health problems and physically limiting conditions.

Medical examinations are for evaluative purposes only, not for treatment.

Psychological status is evaluated by a variety of tests and observational techniques.

Commonly used intelligence tests are individually administered and standardized. Emotional behaviors are measured by direct observations of behavior, standardized tests, scales, and checklists.

Social skills are assessed by the use of such instruments as adaptive behavior scales. These instruments provide information about a child's ability to cope with the natural and social demands of his environment. Like the criterion-referenced tests, these tests identify the specific skills the child possesses.

Caution: Of the frequently used tests, very few are considered by the Authors to be "Good." That is, they provide very little information that can be translated into appropriate instructional programs for children. Tests in the areas of education and psychology often provide a single score that results in a label for the child. Labels usually imply many things that a child is not, and often prevent him/her from receiving a needed service.

Our preference is for the usage of criterion-referenced tests and systematic observational procedures. The observational procedures approach is discussed in **Behavior Disorders: Helping Children With Behavioral Problems** (one of the other books in the Series). These assessment procedures can be translated directly into educational goals for children because they specify the exact behaviors that the child exhibits.

PROTECTION IN EVALUATION PROCEDURES

The law requires that school personnel conduct their evaluations in a nondiscriminatory manner.

Racial and cultural discrimination is specifically mentioned. A nondiscriminatory evaluation is not easy to provide. Guidelines are presented here to help parents and teachers judge whether or not a test is discriminatory.

An intelligence test could be considered discriminatory if the child does poorly because of extenuating circumstances that are not related to the child's intelligence.

The reasons a child may not understand the directions might include impairments in hearing, vision, and language. Sensory problems might cause a child to score poorly on a test, not because of his/her intelligence but rather because of an inability to hear instructions or see the test items.

Likewise unfamiliarity with the English language can cause the child to score poorly. If the child's primary language is not English, the assessment must be in the native language or mode of communication.

If at all possible, the examiner should use the mode of communication used by the child.

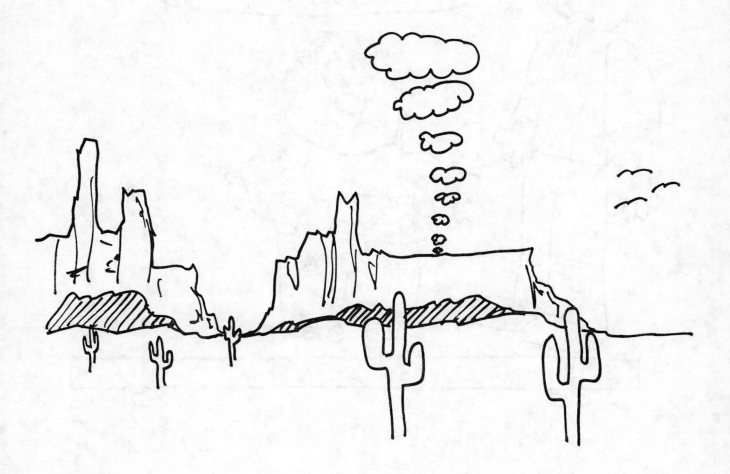

Modes of communication other than oral language might include:

- •Braille;
- •Communication boards; and
- •Sign language or gestures.

Physical problems may also cause a child to do poorly on a test. It is clearly discriminatory to label a child as "retarded" if a physical handicap is the cause of his/her low performance. Children with cerebral palsy would probably score low on most tests of intelligence even though their mental capabilities could be normal or above.

Tests that have been recommended by various professionals as being more or less nondiscriminatory for children with language differences or difficulties are:

- •The Raven's Progressive Matrices;
- •The Draw-A-Person Test; and
- •The Leiter International Intelligence Scale.

It is hard to say, however, that a certain test is nondiscriminatory for a particular child. The best measure of a test's fairness is the extent to which circumstances unrelated to the test cause poor performance.

There may be occasions on which parents are not satisfied with the educational assessment their child received. In such cases they may obtain an independent educational evaluation.

58

ACCESS TO STUDENT RECORDS

Schools are required to permit parents to review the personal school records of their children.

The school should comply with such requests from parents without "unnecessary delay and prior to any hearing related to the identification, evaluation, or placement of the child, and in no case more than 45 days after the request has been made."

Parents have the right to inspect and review educational records.

As part of this right to review their child's records, parents have the right to receive explanations and interpretations of the information and data. If the parents do not understand certain information, disagree with it, or simply want a better understanding of their child's records, they are entitled to review such information and have it meaningfully explained to them.

Parents have the right to receive copies of the records if the records are in a form not easily available for inspection. Some records are stored in computers. Upon request, such information must be made available in written form for parental inspection.

Parents have the right to request changes in the information if they believe that the data are inaccurate, misleading, or in violation of the privacy or other rights of the child.

After the records are no longer needed for educational purposes, they should be destroyed within five years. A permanent record can be kept which includes information such as name, address, phone number, grades, attendance record, classes attended, and grade level completed.

chapter 3

---

serving handicapped children

TRAINING PERSONNEL TO TEACH HANDICAPPED CHILDREN

The Education For All Handicapped Children Act requires that, to the greatest extent possible, handicapped children must be educated with children who are not handicapped. As a result, many mildly handicapped children will be served in regular classes for part of each school day instead of being placed in self-contained special education classes where they are separated from their nonhandicapped peers.

However, most regular class teachers have not been trained to teach handicapped students.

The Act therefore requires that each state develop plans for providing in-service training for general and special education teachers. Without in-service training many teachers will have great difficulty in adequately pro- gramming for handicapped children. With a moderate amount of in-service training the average teacher should be able to adequately provide most of the educational needs of mildly handicapped children.

In-service programs might include:

- how to write an individualized educational program;
- methods and techniques of teaching academic and social behavior;
- educational aspects of various handicapping conditions;
- systematic instruction;
- vocational education for students with special needs;
- resources and services for handicapped students;
- The Right To Education For All Handicapped Children (Public Law 94-142);
- helping children with communication problems;
- counseling exceptional children;
- regular class adjustment of the physically handicapped.

For information about mainstreaming children with specific disabilities, see the other books in this Series listed on the back cover of this book.

Each state must develop methods of informing special education teachers and administrators of significant findings from educational research and demonstration projects, and. . .

. . .adopt, as much as possible, promising educational practices and materials that have been developed through these projects.

INDIVIDUALIZED EDUCATIONAL PROGRAMS

Each handicapped child must have a *written* individualized educational program designed especially for him or her.

Since the advent of mainstreaming, these programs have importance for regular class teachers because they will be partially responsible for implementation. The program should be planned by a Child Study Team which includes a qualified representative of the local education agency, the teacher, the child's parents or guardian, and occasionally...

. . .the child. Although it is uncommon for children to assist in developing their own educational program, it may often be desirable. This involvement is not feasible for young or severely retarded children, but it may be especially appropriate for adolescents to have a part in planning their own education.

If the child has surrogate parents, they have the right to participate in developing the individualized program. They may either approve or disapprove of the program.

The child's parents or guardian *must* be given the opportunity to have a voice in deciding the child's educational future.

They should help make program decisions and will ultimately have to approve the educational program and instructional plan before the school is able to assist the child.

A. The individualized educational program must include the child's present level of educational performance.

The child's present performance level can be determined by a variety of methods including formal and informal tests, systematic observation, and reports from parents, teachers, and other qualified professional personnel.

To know that a child "isn't making it" in a regular class is not sufficient reason to remove him/her from that class. As mentioned earlier, a multi-faceted assessment is required to determine what skills and problems a child has.

B. The individualized educational program must include a statement of annual goals and short-term instructional objectives.

The child study team will decide on the long-term goals for the child. For example, a long-term goal for a severely handicapped child might be that the child will learn to feed him/herself independently.

A second goal might be that the child will learn to dress him/herself. The child study team must state the goals in order of their priority.

Instructional objectives should be included which specify the tasks the child must learn to reach the goal. An instructional objective for the goal of self-feeding might be stated like this:

With a plastic spoon the child will be able to scoop applesauce into the spoon, lift the spoon to his/her mouth, and put it into his/her mouth without spilling on five of six trials.

Long- and short-term goals with their accompanying instructional objectives communicate important information to all who are involved with the child. The goals let us know what the priorities are and provide a base against which we can measure progress. Without these goals we are often left with hearsay and unsubstantial evidence of progress.

WHAT WAS IT WE WERE SUPPOSED TO DO WITH EDDIE?

I DON'T REMEMBER BUT THOSE BLOCKS SHOULD KEEP HIM OCCUPIED FOR SEVERAL WEEKS!

C. The individualized educational program must include the specific educational services to be provided for the child and the extent to which the child will be able to participate in regular education programs.

In the past, a child's programming has often been vaguely described to parents and regular class teachers. All who are involved with the child should know what is happening to him/her. There must be safeguards to prevent any program being an educational dumping area.

D. The individualized educational program must include the projected date for initiation and anticipated duration of special services. These times must be specified because in the past children have often either never received a service or have been placed in a service for years with little or no review of progress.

E. The individualized educational program must include appropriate objective criteria, evaluation procedures and schedules for determining, at least on an annual basis, whether or not instructional objectives are being achieved.

This annual review does not necessarily mean that a child will need to be retested every year. It does mean that the available data should be examined and the following questions should be asked at least once a year: Are the deficits still present? Are the recommended procedures still appropriate? Is the educational setting still appropriate? In many programs these decisions are made much more frequently.

REVIEW

The individualized educational program must include:

1. A statement of the child's present level of educational functioning;

2. A statement of annual goals and short-term objectives;

3. The educational services to be provided and the amount of time the child can be mainstreamed;

4. The date for starting the program and how long it is expected to last; and

5. Objective criteria, evaluation procedures, and schedules for determining whether instructional objectives are being met.

EXAMPLE OF AN INDIVIDUALIZED EDUCATIONAL PROGRAM

Student's Name: Sarah Doe
School: Main Elementary

PRESENT LEVEL OF FUNCTIONING:
Sarah does not complete math assignments; she does not begin assignments on time, and when she does work, she stays on-task for an average of 3 minutes out of 30.

ANNUAL GOALS:
Sarah will complete all required math assignments.

SHORT-TERM OBJECTIVES:
Sarah will begin working on her math within 60 seconds after the teacher tells her to begin working. Sarah will complete the number of math problems assigned within the time allotted by the teacher. Sarah will stay on-task for 25 out of 30 minutes while working on math assignments.

EDUCATIONAL SERVICES TO BE PROVIDED:
Behavior Management Program

AMOUNT OF TIME IN REGULAR CLASS:
80%

STARTING DATE OF PROGRAM:
4-4-77

DURATION OF PROGRAM:
Expected - 6 weeks

OBJECTIVE CRITERIA AND EVALUATION PROCEDURES:
Teacher will keep continuous (daily) objective records of the time between giving the assignment and Sarah's beginning to work, the number of math problems Sarah completes within 30 minutes, and the amount of time Sarah stays on-task during the 30 minute math period.

SERVING CHILDREN IN PRIVATE SCHOOLS

In some cases, depending on the available schools and the nature of a child's handicap, it may be that a private school or institution would be the most appropriate educational setting.

If the local school district so recommends, a child may be placed in such a program.

The private school or institution must be approved by the state education agency.

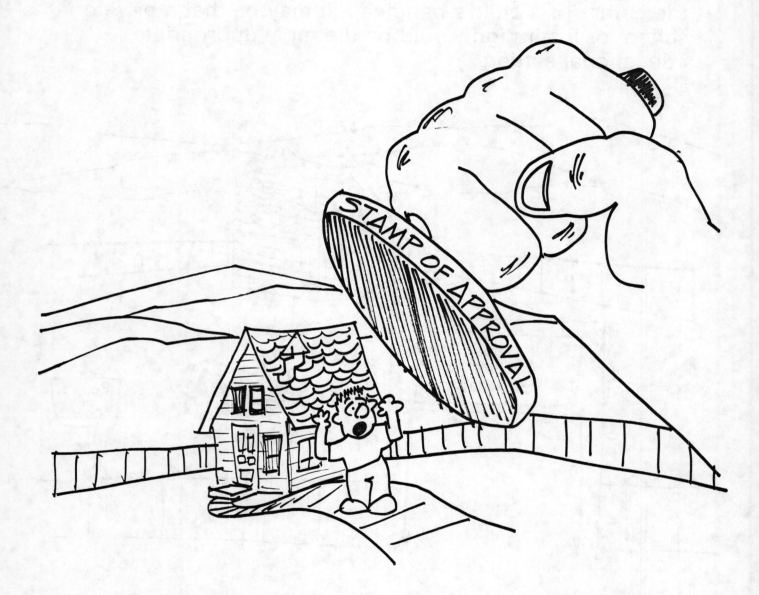

Without this approval the local school agency may not place a child in such a school. If the child is placed in a private school, it must be at no cost to the parents.

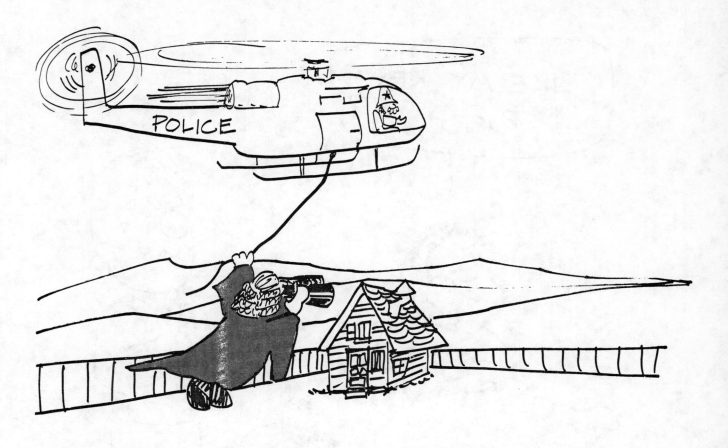

Children placed in state approved private schools or institutions will have all of the same rights and privileges as they would in a public school. The same procedures regarding due process, assessment, and availability of records apply where children in private settings are being served as part of the public school's responsibility.

Children served in private programs by the public schools also have the same rights to an individualized educational program as they would in a public school. In summary, the child has the same rights and privileges as he/she would in a public school.

CONCLUSION

Until very recently, American education has not changed significantly over the past 50 years. It is now in the process of undergoing a dramatic change. The change will be due partly to the joining of forces of two separate movements - integration and individualization. They are both important components of P.L. 94-142.

Integration and mainstreaming are essentially the same. The basic assumption of both is that children should not be removed from the mainstream of education. The mainstreaming movement is not new; it has been around for many years. In the present law, the U.S. Congress has clearly committed itself to the concept.

Individualization is also an important aspect of this law. Handicapped children are required to be provided individualized educational programs. These plans, with their long- and short-term objectives, will greatly assist in bringing appropriate service to children. It has not been uncommon for children to be "dead-ended" in special classes, with little or no attention to the quality of services received. Individualized educational programs will help make teachers more professional and accountable.

This law will not affect special education teachers alone. It will affect all who come into contact with handicapped children. The requirement for education in the least restrictive environment (mainstreaming) will result in nearly all teachers coming into contact with handicapped children. Teachers will see the value that results from providing individualized plans for children and the practice will spread throughout the regular classes.

About the Editor

Thomas N. Fairchild has his Ph.D. in School Psychology and is currently an Assistant Professor of Guidance and Counseling and Coordinator of the School Psychology Training Program at the University of Idaho. Dr. Fairchild earned his Bachelors, Masters, and Specialist degrees at the University of Idaho. He received his Ph.D. from the University of Iowa in 1974. The editor has published over a dozen journal articles in the areas of school psychology and counseling. Dr. Fairchild has worked as a teacher, counselor, and school psychologist. He has had the privilege of working with students across all grade levels, and in his opinion they are all special.

About the Authors

A. Lee Parks is an Associate Professor of Special Education at the University of Idaho. He began his professional career as a school psychologist in the State of Washington. He attended the University of Kansas where he received his Ph.D. During this time he worked as a Research Trainee for the Bureau of Child Research. After receiving his doctorate he accepted a position at The Ohio State University where he held a joint appointment with the Nisonger Center for Mental Retardation and the Faculty for Exceptional Children. He is presently at the University of Idaho.

Marilyn K. Rousseau is presently the Director of Special Services, Department of Mental Health and Mental Retardation in Nashville, Tennessee. She received her Ph.D. in Special Education from Florida State University. Her previous training includes teaching at both the high school and university levels. She taught high school for two years and served as a Lecturer in Educational Psychology at Riverina College of Advanced Education, New South Wales, Australia. She has served as a consultant for the emotionally disturbed, a curriculum consultant, and recently as an Assistant Professor of Special Education at the University of Idaho.

About the Illustrator

Anyone can draw, but to be a good illustrator one must have three things: First, one needs a keen awareness of life in order to keep a running file of personal experiences for future reference; second, one needs a personal style or technique of drawing established and refined by time. For example, the technique of *line economy* is important. This is the knack of creating expressions or poses with a minimum use of line. And third, but most importantly, an illustrator must have *fun* while drawing, for if he does, it will show in his work so that others will enjoy it too.

The illustrator of this book possesses all of these qualities and more. He is Bart Miller, a fourth year Architecture major at the University of Idaho. He works on campus as a graphic artist, but this is his first experience in illustrating books. "I love to draw; especially kids and animals," he says. His major goal is to become an architect, but he also hopes to illustrate a series of children's books. Until then he hopes you enjoy this book.

X